The
4 Step Flip!

Quit your job and never look back.

Maria A. Mendez, MBA

Copyright © 2018 Maria A. Mendez, MBA

ISBN-13 978-1729561836

ISBN-10 978-1729561837

All rights reserved. *No part of this publication may be reproduced or stored in a retrieval system by any means: mechanical, digital, photocopy, recording or any other method except for brief quotations in printed reviews without the prior permission of the author.*

Dedication

As with all of my books, I dedicate this book to my son, Dominic Mendez. You are the most dedicated and loving son that a mother could have. Your actions have gone far beyond what a child should ever be expected to do for a parent. I am so blessed to share my life with you. You have always been there for me and without you, this would not have been possible. I thought I was the one raising you to have a better life, but it was you who provided the better life for me. You were my miracle when you were born and you continue to be my miracle every day!

Acknowledgements

I would like to express my most sincere gratitude to those friends in my life who supported me by encouraging me to keep going, reminding me not to look backwards, ensuring that I did not get lazy and most importantly teaching me to not only to believe that "I can" rather than "I can't", but to also live it.

Contents

Section 1 7

   Introduction 8

Section 2 17

   The 4 F's of Flipping 18

      Find Funding 19

      Find a Property 25

      Fix (Renovate) the Property 28

      Flip (Resell) the Property 31

Section 3 33

   Summary and Conclusion 34

Section 4 37

   Reference Material 38

      Glossary and Acronyms 40

      What Do They Really Mean? 90

      Author Biography 94

      Other Books by the Author 97

      Dedication to Readers 98

The
4 Step Flip!

Quit your job and never look back.

Section 1

Introduction

Flipping real estate has become a phenomenon. Television shows date back beyond a decade at this point, with new ones often showing up but there's a different take on them all. Some shows focus on flips in Vegas, Nashville and Texas while others boast their first time flip experiences. So no matter what you desire, most likely you can find it. The bottom line with the majority of the shows though, is how to find, renovate and resell properties for big bucks. Even though the shows portray the challenges that the flippers experience, there is usually a positive end result by the end of the show.

That isn't always what actually happens though. Every once in awhile, you'll see that someone had to move into their flip because it didn't sell or it had to be sold for less than what was expected. The shows make it seem so easy or easily fixable once a mistake is made. That may be true if a professional is brought in to help out. By providing the basics to get started hopefully that will help you to minimize the possibility of those situations or avoid them completely.

Why is flipping houses so seductive? The promise of being able to make big bucks in a short amount of time of course. There are others as well. People have been saying for years that they want a better work and life balance. This is even more prevalent with the millennials today. In fact, in one survey by EY, it was found that nearly 40% of millennials would consider moving to a different county in order to achieve a better balance in their lives (CNBC).

There have been several attempts by corporations to make good on those requests and many have rolled out their own versions of work life balance, however many of them missed the mark. Why is this? Well, because many of the corporations boast work life balance, but what they mean by it, is that employees are able to work remotely from home. So what happens to those people? They often ended up working in the office and at home, actually putting in even more hours. Granted, while being able to work from home does have some advantages, I am not sure that is what the true intent was particularly since more work is now brought into the family home. I suspect the original intent was to have better quality family time rather than working longer hours regardless of the location of the work.

Those companies that were not able to be as flexible with hours or remote working started rolling out programs with other perks. Some have offered job sharing, flexible work times, condensed work weeks and yet others have offered unlimited time off, or other perks while on site. Some of those perks have included onsite day care, physical therapy, massages, free food, bocce courts, fitness centers, concierge services, rock climbing walls and the list goes on and on according to Business Insider. These programs help with stress reduction, exercise, cutting down on time to run some errands and overall better mental states.

Of course there are companies that do have a true work life balance, but there are exceptions to everything. Still other people want to control their own destiny and work on their own schedules rather than within the parameters that a corporation has decided is best for everyone.

So that brings us back to flipping real estate. This may bring about better work life balance as working as an entrepreneur, *you control your schedule*, for the most part. You'll have the ability to control when you perform online searches to find properties.

You'll have the ability to control when you drive past properties to get a better look. For the most part, you'll be able to control when your realtor shows you properties. You'll be able to control when you shop for materials and when work is completed. So there is an awful lot that will be within your control, but don't forget that when you decide to cut out early because you were frustrated, money be left on the table. Time truly is money in this business and the faster you can get the flip completed, the quicker you'll

arrive at your payday. Is taking the day off or leaving early worth it? Only you can decide that for yourself. Regardless, you will be in control of your schedule and therefore be closer to achieving the work like balance that fits for you and your family. You'll need the dedication and knowledge to be successful.

If you aren't already in the construction field or design field, where do you find the education to get started and is it even necessary? Education teaches us that we should learn how to do something *before* we do it and it also teaches us how to get a job. That's why there are so many programs out there to educate the masses. However, the last time I checked, there wasn't a class in high school or college that teaches people how to flip houses. The education comes from a combination of things such as construction, zoning laws, design, purchasing, accounts payables, project management, relationship management, marketing, sales and so on. In the flipping shows I mentioned earlier, often someone has experience in something such as construction, design or being a real estate agent, but very few have experience in everything. A lot learn as they go, but they could pay the price for the lack of knowledge or experience.

Learning to flip properties is going to teach you a lot more than the how to of the process though. It's going to show you how to take control of your own destiny. It's going to show you that your efforts will be rewarded and it is going to show you how to achieve financial independence. The IRS reported that over the past few years 71% of those with incomes greater than 1 million dollars were in real estate. There is no need to buy into the notion that you should be working from 8am until 5pm daily, 5 days a week for the majority of the year, *for someone else* and hope that the someone else is going to reward you for your efforts. Some will tell you that your paycheck is your reward. I don't see it that way at all. I see the

paycheck as the agreed upon amount to do a certain function. Essentially you are trading your time for a fee. That's a contract, *not* a reward. The reward comes when you're able to achieve financial independence and not have to worry about working paycheck to paycheck like many Americans do today.

Now think about corporate America for a minute. Does everyone know everything? Certainly not. What the best managers do is surround themselves with a team that has varying experience and knowledge and usually different than that of the hiring manager. This allows the team to be stronger and hopefully minimize possible risk. This carries over into flipping real estate. So think about putting your team together and who might complement your knowledge and skills already. Choose a real estate agent that is knowledgeable about the area and processes. Choose an attorney that specializes in real estate and works with a reputable title agency. If you need financing, work with someone who is able to provide approvals on short notice and preferably with the least amount of paperwork or red tape. Choose wisely when deciding on contractors to work with. Ask questions, lots and lots of questions to ensure that the parties will be able to meet your expectations and time lines. So can you get started knowing next to nothing. Absolutely....if you create the right team for yourself.

Since getting started with little to no knowledge might scare some of you, there are ways in which education can be provided. Home Depot offers do-it-yourself classes and they range from how to install backsplashes, to tiles, installing lights or ceiling fans or even toilets. So even if you aren't going to complete the work yourself, it may be a good idea to take a class to determine how difficult the job is and how long it might take. This knowledge will help in negotiations with contractors. If you prefer an even more hands on form of education, there is always the possibility of taking an apprentice job with a contractor. This will not only teach you how to do the work while make some money, but it will also teach you about the challenges and strategies the contractors use. Again, this experience would be invaluable in negotiations in the future.

For the stay at home types, there are multiple books the specifics. YouTube is also an invaluable resource. There are how-to videos on just about everything about there. There are also many seminars that are offered online or in person for free. Even those boast the similar experiences with people saying they have flipped 100's of homes and on average 30 in a one month period of time. A lot of the seminars will provide just enough information, most of which is common sense, to get people interested, but then at the end of the presentation or seminar, the real goal is revealed. They are seeking a limited amount of people to be part of their inner circle and share their flipping secrets with. The "advantages" come in all different forms. Sometimes, it's private one on one time with the expert presenter or his or her chosen few. Other times it is access to lists of private lenders willing to lend their funds to you so you don't have to use your own funds. Of course, all of these "secrets" in the inner circle come with a price which is often somewhere around the $1000 range. So take the information you can get for free then decide whether the "fee" is something you want to pay.

Why are the seminars so enticing? People don't want to use their own funds or don't have their own funds to get involved in flipping houses so of course, using someone else's funds will make this much easier for some or even possible for others. So the hefty $1000 price tag may not seem all that hefty in the bigger scope of things especially if that list of magic people will be provided. Trust me, with a little help from Google, you can probably find the same information yourself!

Training can also be acquired. A typical real estate agent class is relatively inexpensive at only about $500 for a duration of about 6 weeks. Don't have the construction knowledge? There are classes to become home inspectors. Those classes also range widely in time frame as they can be anywhere from about 12 hours of classes with 40 hours in the field and on up to a year of training. The cost is about $2000. These classes certainly won't make you a general contractor, but they will provide more knowledge than most people have when starting out. Even the right contacts can help. A good realtor and good contractor can be of tremendous assistance.

It's also a good idea to learn the lingo so people will know that you know what you're talking about. There's a lot of acronyms that'll be discussed in regard to the flipping portion of this business, but keep in mind there's also specific language that contractors will use. The more familiar you are with the lingo, the less likely it will be that someone will try to take advantage of you with higher prices or work that is not up to "snuff".

The basics of flipping homes are simple. That's exactly what this book is going to show you. As I indicated, there are multiple shows on television that boast the "how to" of flipping homes and each has its own spin on the process. Some flip homes to bring life back into dilapidated properties. Some flip homes to help bring people to areas that are expected to be up and coming. Some flip homes with friends and others alone. The one thing in common is they all flip to make money and they all follow the same basic steps. The basics are all just that....the basics. There are 4 steps that fit into the basics.

1. *Find Funding.*

2. *Find a property.*

3. *Fix or Renovate the property.*

4. *Flip or Resell the property.*

Otherwise known as the 4 F's of Flipping: Fund, Find, Fix and Flip!

Sounds fairly easy and straight forward, right? 4 Steps doesn't sound too bad at all. Flipping properties will allow you to take control of your work schedule, your work life balance and ultimately your future. **You could have the option to quit your job and never look back.** Flipping even works on smaller scales. Flipping can be used to pay off student loans, pay off credit card debt, fund your IRA accounts, fund your investment accounts, save for your children's college education or even save for that well deserved vacation or a vacation home. As long as you know the basics, you'll have a great foundation to start from. If this is your plan, stick to it and you'll do just fine. So let's see what is involved in each step.

Section 2

4 F's of Flipping!

Find Funding

Find a Property

Fix the Property

Flip the Property

FIND FUNDING.

In order to purchase a property, cash will be needed. Cash comes through a variety of methods, but the most obvious are from your own bank accounts or investment accounts, taking loans out from banks, credit cards, borrowing from friends or family or private lenders. So flippers will need to have their own sources of cash, have a network of people with cash who are willing to lend it out or have sufficient credit to be able to obtain cash from the banks through one method or another.

So let's start with your bank account. Have you saved sufficient money to be able to buy a house, renovate it and hold it until it's sold and closed? Arguably, this is the cheapest and easiest way to fund your flip. The rates that the banks are offering are very low at about 1%, at the time of this writing, for an average savings account. So pulling your funds out of those savings accounts, that aren't doing much for you anyway, might be an option. Weigh the possible return from the potential flip against what you're making by leaving your funds in the bank to earn interest to see if this would be a viable option for you. In most cases, I would bet the answer would be yes. For future reference, a copy of the bank statement showing the proof of funds or available funds for the home purchase should be sufficient.

The next option is to pull funds from your investment accounts which could include your stocks or mutual funds. This is going to widely vary from one person to another as everyone's risk tolerance is different. Therefore, the cost of pulling funds out from your stocks or mutual funds is going to be different for everyone. According to CNBC, the average returns on US stocks in 2016 was about 10.33%. So by pulling your funds out of your investment account, the cost may be about 10% if the investments remain equal for the following year. Those earnings from your investments should be considered when deciding to pull funds from your investments. You would need to get a return on your funds of at least this just to break even. For future reference, you should be able to show that you have funds available in your investment account before actually liquidating them to make the purchase.

One of the other possible investments that could be a viable option is your 401k account. There's the ability to withdraw funds from those accounts, however the withdrawal comes at a cost too. In addition to paying federal and state taxes on the funds, there would also be a 10% penalty for early withdrawal if you are under the age of 59 1/2 (irs.gov).

There's a possibly second option with a 401k account. If you check the terms of your 401k, there may be an option to borrow funds against the account and pay the account back, with interest of course. The ability to borrow will depend on the employer and the terms of the account. Also, if you have a solo 401k, the same goes for these accounts. Either your account has to be set up with the ability to borrow against it or the account needs to be held with an investment organization that allows the account to be borrowed against. If your account is with an employer, chances are they will determine the amount of interest that'll need to be repaid and they'll dictate the terms offered. There are limitations to the amounts being taken out as well. This will tie to the amount of funds in the account and IRS regulations in the US. Always check with your local government to see what the requirements may be. If the 401k account is a solo account, then you will be able to determine the amount of interest and repayment terms. They may need to be approved by the investment institution holding the account though. One advantage with the 401k loan is that the

interest that's paid, is paid back to your own 401k account. Therefore, you're acting as your own bank. This is an advantage as rather than paying someone else the interest, it gets paid back to you! This is the only option that has this detail worked directly into it. You may be able to show the balance or 401k loan application in order to view listings, but always check with your agent as to the expectations.

There are also some options to borrow funds from banks in one form or another. Since flip properties often need to be purchased with cash, a traditional mortgage isn't usually an option. However, there are other options such as personal loans or home equity loans. There may be collateral tied to these options though such as your primary home or other assets that you may have already. Banks will likely ask what the plan is for the use of the funds and since flipping properties is risky, the application may take some finesse. With the home equity option, the bank could be more willing to lend the funds as they will mostly likely be protected with your primary home as collateral. This process would mostly likely include an appraisal on the primary residence and take longer to obtain than the options previously discussed, but with some planning, this could be a viable option for obtaining funding for a flip. When borrowing from banks, the funds will either need to be in your account or in the case of a home equity line, showing that there is available credit to draw on may be sufficient to see listings.

Next are those pesky credit cards. You spent your life building up credit and have credit cards with higher limits that probably aren't being utilized. So why not take advantage of the credit you built up and use them to make the purchase or finance the renovations? This may take some finessing as well and may end up costing too much if not done properly. Most places don't allow the purchase of a property directly on a credit card. Therefore, a cash advance may need to be taken and with rates ranging anywhere from about 9% and up currently with most of them at almost double this rate if not more, this could get to be very expensive very quickly and of course cut into your profit margin. This option may also have an adverse result to your credit report and score as your revolving balances would be higher suddenly. With a drop in a credit score, there is the possibility that nothing further would get approved until the credit score goes back up. So keep that in mind.

There's also the ability to transfer funds on different apps out there if you look around. They usually charge a small fee of about 2.9% or 3% of a transaction which on a $30,000 transaction may run about $900, but this could be a small price to pay to get your hands on funds. Of course I am not suggesting that you go into debt beyond your means, just letting you know what some people have done in order to get started. It all is going to fall on your risk tolerance and what is available to you. For the credit cards, the realtors may take a copy of the statement showing what the available credit is and that it is in your name in order to be able to see properties.

Another possibility is borrowing funds from friends or family. In some cases this may result in low cost loans since the people already know you. In other cases, it may mean higher interest rates, again because they know you! Borrowing from friends and family brings a whole new slew of issues into play though. If you're successful and they provided a low cost loan, they may feel some resentment that you walked away with a nice profit and they were paid hardly anything. Or if the flip is not successful and they have to wait longer to get their funds returned, there could be hard feelings or even more resentment. No one wants to sit around dinner at holiday time when there were money issues in a family. It would just be uncomfortable for all involved. If things go well, you may have a lender for the next project or possibly a partner though. There's no way of knowing ahead of time how it would turn out. As far as the project itself, details would need to be ironed out ahead of time. Would the friend or family member be able to have final say on the property? The design? The contractors hired? The resale price? Acceptance of bids? There's a lot to think about if this option is chosen. For friends and family, the funds should need to be borrowed and deposited into an account in your name before viewings are allowed. Keep in mind that not all agents will operate the same way so always check with your local jurisdiction for laws or regulations as well as your realtor to determine what is acceptable as proof of funds.

The final basic way to obtain funds is through the use of private lenders. These lenders typically will lend money starting at 4% or more at the time of this writing. Many won't touch a flip unless they are receiving 10-12% or more. Private lenders will often have liens put on your flip property so they can protect their investment. So they do act much like a bank. These lenders also usually want to know about the project including details of how it will be improved and what your expected resale value will be. Some will approve or deny the request within 24-72 hours after the application is received which is fairly quick. Terms are also negotiable with private lenders so start thinking about the repayment and whether it is a good idea to agree to a principal and interest repayment. It may be a better idea to work an interest only repayment until sale or even better yet no payment until the close on the property after it is repaired. Private lenders often won't lend funds until the flipper has at least 3 flips under his or her belt and often under the same name. So if you flipped one property in your personal name and then decided to flip another in a business name, they may look at it as only have completed 1 flip. So ask a lot of questions so you know exactly what the expectations are going to be. The private lenders will provide a proof of funds letter so that you are able to view listings and put bids into the sellers.

Now you know that funding is easier than you may have expected, several options are available and *not having cash up front may no longer be an issue*. So weigh the options to determine which one or combination is going to work best for you and then get out there and make it happen! This is step 1 of being able to possibly leave your day job and start flipping as a career.

FIND A PROPERTY.

Now that the decision was made about how the project is going to be funded, it's time to move forward and actually find a property to flip. This has always been one of my favorite parts of the flipping process. If you're like me, you'll like to find the diamond in the rough and get excited about the project and the possibilities. If you can find the ugliest house on the best street, that is a great start! This brings excitement to the project. After all, you should love what you're doing and how many of us can say that today?! Two of the most basic ways to find properties are to use the Multiple Listing Service (MLS) or buy from an auction. Both come with their own set of advantages and disadvantages.

The most obvious and easiest way to locate a property is by looking online and both the MLS listings and the auctions can be found online these days. This makes it a lot easier today than in the past. Most sites are set up to allow basic search criteria such as the price, square footage, number of bedrooms, number of bathrooms and area to be entered, which will make this task much easier. The MLS is what the real estate agents use to enter their listings and the MLS feeds the other sites available for searches. So put in your criteria and narrow your search. The sites will provide a multitude of information about the property itself such as square footage, number of bedrooms and bathrooms, type of heating, whether there is basement or garage, style of home, possible historical facts and other pertinent details. The sites also usually include other helpful information such as taxes, school districts and their ratings, local crime, prior sales, the neighborhood, home expenses, possible price of improvements. Although, a word of caution, always check the facts provided as they can often contain outdated or inaccurate data. However, it is a great starting place. Once you have a few selections, choose a real estate agent to ensure you will have access to the property. Happy Hunting.

The second most common option to find a property is through the use of an auction. Bargains could be found through this method very easily. Some auctions are held online and others in person. Very often they sell a property on a given day so your chances of getting a good deal are high as not everyone is going to be able to show up to the auction at the designated time. There is usually a small deposit with the balance due a short time afterwards. There are also some cons to buying a property at an auction. There are often reserves set which are minimum amounts that the seller is willing to accept. Of course the reserve amount is not usually disclosed so it may not be realized until the end of the auction. Also, there is limited time to get inspections competed, if allowed at all. Sometimes, access to the property isn't granted so the interior can't even be viewed. This is very risky for obvious reasons. Potentially you could get into a property and have no idea how to budget the projects since you are unable to determine the amount of work that will be needed until the property is changed over to you. There could also be title issues such as outstanding liens or unpaid utility bills that are unresolved at the time of the sale and those title issues would need to be resolved by the purchaser before the property could be resold. Don't forget about those buyer's premiums which are usually about 5%. Now that you've decided what properties to view, contact a real estate agent to gain access to the properties. Don't be shy. Ask questions. The realtor may be able to obtain information that is not readily available to you. Be prepared when you go to the viewings as you never know what's going to be in these properties. Comfortable, safe footwear is a start. You may also need a mask or breathing machine to prevent mold or other things from getting into your lungs. Always take a flashlight, camera and something to take notes with at the very least. This will help if you're seeing multiple properties. Don't forget to check outside as well as inside. Since the house may be a foreclosure or sitting vacant for some time, be sure to check and see if mechanicals are still in tact.

Now that you've been able to see some properties or obtained one through an auction, put your bid in and got it accepted, next choose your real estate attorney. Once you have found your dream project, your agent will coordinate the paperwork with your attorney and should help get you through the process until the closing on the property at which time, you'll get the keys to the property and more fun will start! This is step 2 in the process and this can be done with little to no knowledge. So again, this is very viable for someone new to the game. You're another step closer to leaving that day job!

FIX (RENOVATE) THE PROPERTY.

Congratulations you have a property! By this time you have either already seen the property at least once with a realtor or possibly this is your first look at the interior of the property if it was purchased through an auction. The goal is to come up with a solid game plan of the repairs that are necessary and the updates that you would like to put into the property. This may be done with or without your contractor, if you are going to use one. I like to go through a property again myself first to see if there's anything I missed and make a list before meeting with the contractor(s). Then walk through again with the contractor(s) to discuss the plans. They may tell you that it would be more costly to do what you planned or have other ideas for you. It's a good idea to have a list of what was talked about and the estimated price as well so it's fair and enforceable by both parties.

Choosing a contractor is a critical part of the renovation if you're going to use one rather than completing all of the work independently. They are definitely not all created equally and definitely don't charge the same amount. You'll need to find someone you're comfortable working with, that you trust, that does good work and is affordable. Knowing the lingo is important as well. Otherwise the price may go up because they'll think that you don't know what you're doing. Also, research the pricing for jobs so you know what the market dictates from the low to high end so you can have a more educated discussion with your contractors.

Some flips will be easy and entail just paint and carpets or minor repairs. If you find one like this, you're very lucky and probably one of the very few. Most of the properties out there in this arena that have the most profit potential are foreclosed properties. In the WNY area, these houses usually sit vacant for 3 years or more and through the harsh winters, that can do a number on the house and the mechanics. The more complicated flips will involve new plumbing, new gas lines, updated electrical, new layouts, flooring, new drywall and redesign in general. Are you going to handle the design yourself or bring a designer in? If you are brining a designer in, now is the time so they know what they are working with. Let the designer know about your plans to change things so they are able to incorporate the changes into their design plan as well. Always include a buffer in your renovation budget to allow for the unseen and unknown and don't forget about the sweat equity. The more work you're able to do on your own, the more profit will be in your pocket, provided you can work quickly. If it takes you 2 weeks to finish what a contractor can do in one day, weigh the difference in the cost of the time to determine if the sweat equity is the correct option for that project.

 Once your plan is decided upon, time for demo and shopping! Either you can purchase your materials or the contractor can provide materials and labor with your input on design of course. Chances are you'll get charged for the contractor's time in line and time to shop as well as mark ups on the materials. So factor that in as well. Come up with a project plan including a time line. It is best to work in adjustments if the budget is blown or the project falls behind. You should know the approximate time line of the project before even asking the contractor to ensure they will be able to work on your schedule. What I like to do is include a bonus if they are able to stay on budget and on the time line. This provides extra incentives with no extra work and yet my budget and time line are adhered to.

Decide whether you will provide keys to the property to the contractor or if you will be on site every day. If you're working with someone new, I would suggest being at the property. Once you have established a relationship that could change down the road. Once everything is agreed to and in writing, it's time to get the work completed. Schedule inspections to ensure the project plan is coming along as expected, on time and on budget. Be available for your contractor or decisions may be made without your consent. As the project comes closer to the end, you may want to invite your realtor back in to see if he or she has any opinions about making last minute changes. After all, the realtor knows what the buyers are currently looking for and is in the best position to advise you on those things. Be ready for long days and long hours, but also keep in mind that manual labor can be taxing on a body and overworking your contractors may lead to them taking time off or not providing the highest quality work. Always be ready for the unexpected! This is step 3 in the process. This is the part that will take the most knowledge. So if you don't have the knowledge or experience, be sure find some education or find someone who does have the knowledge and experience. You're now on your 3rd step from possibly walking away from that day job!

FLIP (RESELL) THE PROPERTY.

Now that the work is completed, time to get the property back on the market and get it sold. Don't forget to clean up though. There are 2 basic options for resale: selling it on your own or using a realtor. There are advantages and disadvantages to both options. Either way, your profit awaits you at closing, so choose the best option and get it sold!

If you choose to sell the property on your own, you'll save the commissions paid out to a realtor which is usually about 6% of your selling price which could amount to about $6000 on a sale of $100,000 or $12,000 on a sale of $200,000 or $30,000 on a sale of $500,000. Those commissions can add up pretty quickly if the property is worth a lot. This will also mean that you'll need to hold your own open houses, do the marketing, go to the showings to let people in and see the property and handle the paperwork. So determine if you're ready to pay the price or do all of the work yourself.

If you aren't ready for this just yet, then choose a real estate agent skilled in sales. Just because you used one agent for the purchase doesn't mean they are the best option to sell the property. Interview a few and see who you might want to work with. See what their skill set is and how it will benefit you. Ask how many sales that they had that year or in their career versus acting as a buyer agent. It always makes me leery if the selling agent says the house will sell itself and granted the buyer's agents end up doing a lot more of the selling since they are the ones going through the properties with the potential buyers, but that's no excuse. I would want an agent that is going to communicate to me what is going on, discuss sales and marketing strategy and not just rely on putting it on line and throwing a lockbox on the handle. If that's the case, you may want to try a different agent or resort to selling it yourself. Then again, maybe you want an agent to handle everything and not let you know what is going on unless you need to do something. The realtors get paid to handle the stress, right?

I have always used an agent myself so far, but I have never relied on them to do 100% of the marketing. In my view, the property is mine so I will also advertise on whatever avenue I am able to do so to try and strum up more potential buyers and interest. I've used social media and real estate groups to attract attention. The only problem with this is getting feedback or reliable buyers. Through the agents, the buyers are usually vetted with pre-approval letters and proof of funds whereas posting in groups, anyone can provide feedback and ask questions. This could result in some wasted time. I always direct inquiries to get pre-approvals if they need financing before directing them to my agent. This helps both of us.

This is your turn to be patient and wait for bids to come in. Once an acceptable bid comes in and you accept it, the paperwork goes off to the attorneys to work toward closing and getting your money out of the property. Don't get too excited yet though. My realtor always likes to say that the deal isn't done until the cash is in the pocket. Of course there may be contingencies, inspections, appraisals and more due diligence if the buyers is using a first time home buyer program that may come into play. A good agent will help work through those things so you aren't alone. Once you reach the closing, you reach your pay day and all of your hard work will pay off. Now it's time to find a new flip! Wasn't that easier than you thought it would be?

Section 3

Summary and Conclusion

You now know the 4 basic steps to flipping real estate: find funding, find a property, fix it and flip it! This has put you in an ideal place to leave your day job and never look back! In the reference section you'll also see and learn some of the definitions, acronyms and lingo that are used in real estate and flipping properties. That'll help make you sound like an expert on your very first flip.

This is about as simple as it gets and with great risks come the opportunities for great rewards. A savings account may get you a 1% return on your investment. An investment portfolio may get you about 7%-10% currently. Flipping a house could bring a lot more return on your investment. If you purchased a house for $30,000 and put $25,000 in renovations into it then resold it for $110,000 assuming about $15,000 for closing, holding and commissions then the return on your investment would be about 57%. I even know some experienced flippers that have a returns around 80%. That is significantly higher than the other options we discussed. This is a relatively modest example as well, since home prices in the WNY area are typically much less than of other areas. Therefore, this is a fantastic return on investment and this is why so many people are trying their hand at flipping properties.

As you start to flip properties, you'll learn something new with each one. No mater how many you've completed, rest assured, there'll always be something new to learn! The more knowledge you have, the more prepared you'll be and that can only help you succeed! Always use the wisdom you have. Know that with every step you take in this process that you'll gain more wisdom. Exercise common sense. Do your due diligence and act in an honest manner with integrity.

Even after reading this book, you'll need to keep your knowledge current so always be aware and updated as things are always changing. If you would like a more in depth look at flipping properties and the process, be on the look out for my next book "Flipping Secrets" What No One Tells You About Flipping Real Estate. I will be sharing lessons, horror stories and well information that isn't readily available in other trainings out there today. Happy Flipping!

Section 4

Reference Material

https://www.cnbc.com/2017/05/03/the-20-best-companies-for-work-life-balance.html

https://www.forbes.com/sites/kathryndill/2016/07/29/the-best-companies-for-work-life-balance-3/#3b7f7fed64cf

http://www.businessinsider.com/companies-with-awesome-perks-payscale-2013-1#3m-company-helps-its-employees-to-lose-weight-stop-smoking-and-manage-stress-13

http://www.us.hsbc.com/1/2/home/personal-banking/mortgages/glossary

http://www.housingnyc.com

http://www.cnbc.com/2017/01/04/most-investors-didnt-come-close-to-beating-the-sp-500.html Tom Anderson 1/5/17

http://irs.gov

http://www.realestateabc.com/glossary/

https://www.nar.realtor/auction

https://ny.curbed.com/2017/4/5/15192564/affordable-new-york-421-a-revival

http://www.homeny.org/

https://www.fhfa.gov/DataTools/Tools/Pages/Conforming-Loan-Limits-Map.aspx

http://www.dictionary.com/

Glossary and Acronyms

There are many acronyms and abbreviations used in real estate. In addition, there's lingo that's used in some areas that doesn't pertain to others and this is common in New York City. This is certainly not an exhaustive list as things are always changing and it is meant to provide general information and guidelines. In addition, there are several terms that are included that relate to renting, condominiums, co-ops and lending that could be of assistance. Always consult an attorney in your area regarding current legal definitions.

203 K: Special type of first time home buyers lending program that allows you to combine the cost of the property with the renovation costs and treat the deal as one loan.

3B/1B: Common acronym defining the number of bedrooms versus the number of bathrooms. In this example, there are 3 bedrooms and 1 bathroom.

421-A: The 421-a tax incentive program was created in 1971 to encourage housing development and was recently brought back to life. Under the program, developers of apartment buildings on vacant or underutilized lots throughout the boroughs in NYC receive a temporary exemption from property tax on the value added to the site by new construction. Tax breaks are expected to last for 35 years provided that anyone using the program maintain rent regulated apartments for 40 years (curbed.com).

Abatement: A common legal term meaning the removal, or diminishment of something.

Absorption Rate: The rate at which homes are sold during a given period of time.

Abstract of Title: A historical summary of the recorded instruments and proceedings on the title of a property.

Addendum: An additional item or change beyond the standard.

Adjustable Rate Mortgage or ARM: A loan that has a varying interest rate and payment based on an adjustment period. The adjustment is dependent on the variation in a benchmark index, which would depend on the financial institution.

Adjusted Sales Price: The price on the contract less all credit concessions by the seller.

Affidavit: A written statement of confirmation.

Agent: A real estate buyer's agent, a real estate seller's agent or a broker.

Air Rights: The legal ability to use or control the space above a property. Air rights can be sold, rented or leased to another party.

Amenities: The enhancements that buildings offer its owners or tenants. These usually include a doorman, fitness room, garage, game room, lounge, pool, hot tub, etc.

Amortization: Periodic payment of principal and interest on a liability.

Annual Percentage Rate or APR: The actual effective rate of interest charged on a loan expressed on a yearly basis.

Appraisal: The evaluation of the value of a property by a licensed appraiser. **Appreciation:** Represents an increase in the market value of a property.

Assessment: Value of a property determined by the taxing authority in that area that taxes are based on.

Asset: Something that is owned that has value.

Assignment: The process by which a right or contract is transferred from one party to another

Assumable Mortgage or Financing: Financing arrangement in which the outstanding mortgage and its terms are transferred from the current owner to the buyer.

Attorney: Person who will represent you in legal matters. For real estate, choosing one that specializes in real estate and focuses his or her business on it would be beneficial.

Attorney-in-Fact: A person appointed to perform legal acts for another under a power-of-attorney.

Balloon Mortgage: A short-term mortgage with fixed installments of principal and interest that do not fully amortize the loan. The balance of the mortgage is due in a larger lump sum at the end of the term.

Board Approval: A condition in the standard cooperative sales contract requiring that the buyer obtain approval from the board of directors of the cooperative corporation as a prerequisite to completing the sale.

Bridge Loan: A loan for a short time and can be used when the purchase of one property is dependent on the equity from another property that has not yet been sold. The loan is paid when the property is sold.

Broker: A specialized real estate agent employed on a fee or commission basis as an agent to bring buyers and sellers together and assist in negotiating real estate contracts between them. A broker has continued his or her education beyond the requirement of a real estate agent and is also able to work independently or have agents working for them.

Brownstone: A townhouse that is usually a 3 to 5 story building single family or multi family apartment.

Building Restrictions: The requirements in building codes that affect the size and appearance of the building.

Buy Down: The voluntary paying of discount points by a borrower to reduce mortgage interest rate at the time the loan is made.

Buyer's Broker: A broker who represents the buyer in a real estate purchase.

By-Laws: The rules by which the cooperative corporation or condominium operates.

C.M.A.: Acronym for Comparable Market Analysis. Process of using similar neighborhood homes to determine the possible resale or market value of a property.

C.O.E.: Acronym for "closed of escrow".

Capital Expenditure: An improvement that will last one year or more and increasing the value of the property.

Capital Gain: The seller's gain on an asset used in a trade or business or for investment, including real estate. This gain is taxed at varying rates depending on whether the asset was held for more or less than one year.

Capital Improvement: An item that adds value to the property, adapts the property to new uses, or prolongs the life of property not including maintenance.

Capitalization Rate: The percentage of the investment the investor will receive back each year from the net income from the property.

Caps: Caps are percentage restrictions on an ARM which limit the amount the interest rate may change per year and over the life of the loan.

Carry-Cost Rule: Used by financial institutions (could vary from one to another) to evaluate borrowers for loans. It gives the maximum percentage of a borrower's income that the bank will find acceptable to carry the loan and related housing costs. This rule is used in conjunction with the debt/equity ratio.

Cash Flow: The income produced by an investment property after deducting operating expenses and debt.

Cash Reserve: Requirement of some lenders in a mortgage commitment to have buyers have their accounts funded at the time of the closing for a predetermined number of months of the cost of principal, interest, taxes, and insurance.

Caveat: A warning or caution that may be an amendment to a contract of sale.

Caveat Emptor: "Let the buyer beware". Do your due diligence.

Certificate of Occupancy or C of O: A certificate issued by a local governmental entity responsible for the use of land in the community where the property is located stating that the structures on the property or any improvements made to these structures comply with the codes, ordinances and regulations of that governmental entity and that they may be occupied.

Certificate of Title Opinion: A report based on a title examination, which states the examiner's opinion of the quality of a title to real property.

Cession Deed: Used to relinquish real property to a municipality for a road or other public work project.

Chain: A land measurement of 66 feet.

Chain of Title: A successive conveyance of title to a specific parcel of land.

Chattel: Personal property.

Civil Rights Act of 1866: The Civil Rights Act of 1866 is a federal law that prohibits all discrimination on the basis of race.

Civil Rights Act of 1964: The Civil Rights Act of 1964 is a federal law that prohibits discrimination in many instances, but in Title VI it prohibits discrimination on the ground of race, color, or national origin under any program or activity receiving federal financial assistance.

Civil Rights Act of 1968 or Fair Housing Act of 1968: The Fair Housing Act of 1968 is a federal act prohibiting discrimination in the sale, rental or financing of housing on the basis of race, color, religion, gender or national origin. Also note that your local jurisdictions may have even more specific outlines. Always check with your local authority. In the WNY area, Buffalo, Hamburg, West Seneca and Niagara Falls are just a few examples (Housing Opportunities Made Equal).

Closing: When the transfer of ownership of a property from the seller to the buyer occurs.

Closing Costs: The expenses incurred in the purchase and sale of real property paid at the closing. Some examples are title insurance, attorney fees, appraisal fees, recording fees and taxes.

Closing Disclosure or CD: The final details about the mortgage loan including terms.

Closing Statement: An accounting of the funds received and distributed in a real estate transaction.

Cluster Zoning: Cluster zoning is a form of zoning that provides for several different types of land use within a zoned area rather than a lot by lot basis.

Coastal Zone Management Program: A voluntary program between the federal government and US Coastal and Great Lakes states to address coastal issues.

Co-Broke: An arrangement between two brokerage firms to share a commission. Normally used when one broker is the seller's exclusive listing agent and the other broker represents the buyer.

Code of Ethics: A standard of conduct required by license laws and by the National Association of Realtors.

Codicil: A supplement or an appendix to a will either adding or changing a bequest.

Collateral: The security put up in exchange for a loan, which can be taken by the bank if the loan goes unpaid.

Combination: Refers to when an owner combines two adjoining apartments into one to enhance the value and the space.

Commercial Zones: Zones allowing usage for retail stores, restaurants, hotels and service businesses.

Commission: The payment or percentage to the broker for his or her efforts on marketing and selling the property.

Commission Split: The sharing of commissions between the listing agent and the broker of the buyer.

Commitment Fee: A fee paid to the lender for processing, underwriting and originating the mortgage. It is also known as an origination fee.

Commitment Letter: A letter issued by the lender to the applicant that states funds will be provided subject to written terms and conditions.

Common Area or Common Elements: The area in the property or in the building that is available for use by all owners and tenants.

Common Charge: The monthly charge levied by a condominium to cover the cost of maintaining the common areas and services.

Common Law: The law set by judicial precedent or tradition as contrasted with a written statute.

Common Law Dedication: An act by an owner allowing the public use of a property.

Comparables/Comps/CMA or Comparative Market Analysis: Comps are used in assessing or establishing the fair market value of a property using information from a property that has been sold recently that is similar in size, condition, location and amenities.

Compensatory Damage: The amount of money actually lost, which will be awarded by a court in case of a breached contract.

Competent Parties: Persons or organizations legally qualified to manage their own affairs, including entering into contracts.

Complete Performance: The execution of a contract by virtue of all parties having fully performed all terms.

Condemnation: The exercise of the power of eminent domain or taking private property for public use. Typically seen when a structure is dangerous to enter.

Condemnation Value: The market value of condemned property.

Condition: Is any fact or event which, if it occurs or fails to occur, automatically creates or extinguishes a legal obligation.

Condominium or Condo: A building in which ownership has been partitioned into unit interests. Each apartment owner receives a unit deed and owns an individual unit, but common areas are shared with the other unit owners of the building.

Condominium Declaration: The document that, when recorded, creates a condominium and is also known as a master deed.

Conforming Loan: A mortgage issued within the framework of FNMA/FHLMC (Fannie Mae/Freddie Mac) guidelines in terms and amount which as of 2017 has a maximum value of $424,100 (refer to fafh.gov for map of alternate values based on exact location).

Consideration: Anything of value, as recognized by law, offered as an inducement to contract.

Construction Loan or Mortgage: A short-term loan to obtain funds to construct an improvement.

Constructive Eviction: Constructive eviction results from some action or inaction by the landlord that renders the premises unsuitable for the use agreed to in a lease or other rental contract.

Constructive Notice: Constructive notice occurs when one of any affected parties are bound by the knowledge of a fact even though they have not been officially notified of such fact.

Contingency : A condition in a contract relieving a party of liability if a specified event occurs or fails to occur.

Contract: A legally binding agreement between two parties, and in order to have a valid Contract of Sale in real estate there must be: an offer, an acceptance, competent parties, consideration, legal

purpose, written documentation, description of the property, and signatures of the principals.

Contract Buyer's Policy: The title insurance that protects the contract buyer against defects in contract seller's title.

Contract for Deed: A contract of sale and a financing instrument wherein the seller agrees to convey title when the buyer completes the purchase price installment payments

Contract Rent: The amount agreed to in a lease.

Contract Vendee Sale: A transaction in which a seller transfers beneficial rights, including the right of possession and obligations of ownership, to the purchaser and agrees to close at a future date under definite terms. Ownership can be transferred for tax purposes prior to the transfer of title.

Conventional Mortgage Loan: A loan in which the federal government does not insure or guarantee payment to the lender, but is under the amount of a jumbo mortgage.

Conversion: A conversion is a change in ownership status as from a rental to a condominium.

Convertible Apartment: A one or two bedroom apartment that has space to make another bedroom by construction of a wall inclusive of a window.

Conveyance: The transfer of title to real property.

Cooling-off Period: A three-day right of rescission for certain loan transactions.

Cooperative or Co-op: A building owned by a corporation in which each apartment is allocated shares of stock as well as a proprietary lease. The amount of shares owned is determined by the value and size of the apartment. The cooperative building owns all of the units and the purchaser is buying stock in the corporation or the building.

Co-ownership: Title to real property is held by two or more persons at the same time and is also known as concurrent ownership

Cost Approach: An appraisal method for estimating the value of properties that have few, if any, comparables and are not income-producing.

Counter-offer: A new offer made by either the buyer or seller when rejecting a previous offer.

Covenant: A promise made in writing.

Covenant Against Encumbrances: A promise in a deed that the title does not cause encumbrances except those set forth in the deed.

Covenant for Further Assurances: A promise in a deed that the grantor will execute further assurances that may be reasonable or necessary to perfect the title in the grantee.

Covenant of Quiet Enjoyment: A promise in a deed or lease that the grantee or lessee will not be disturbed in the use of the property because of a defect in the grantor's or lessor's title or lease.

Covenant of Right to Convey: A promise in a deed that the grantor has the legal capacity to convey the title.

Covenant of Seisin: A promise in a deed ensuring the grantee that the grantor has the title being conveyed.

Covenant of Warranty: A promise in a deed that the grantor will defend the title against lawful claimants.

Credit Agency: The company or companies that collect and summarize credit data.

Credit Report: The report put out by the credit agency detailing an individual's credit history, creditors, inquiries, past addresses and payment history.

Credit Score: A numerical rating provided on a credit report that establishes creditworthiness based upon a person's past credit, payment history and their current credit standing.

Cubic-foot Method: A means of estimating reproduction or replacement cost, using the volume of the structure.

Cumulative-use Zoning: A type of zoning permitting a higher priority use even though it is different from the type of use designated for the area.

D.R.: Acronym for "dining room".

Debt-to-Equity Ratio: Also referred to as the loan-to-value ratio, is a method to determine financial leverage.

Debt Service: The cost of carrying a loan, usually through monthly payments of interest and principal.

Debt-to-Income Ratio or Debt-Service Ratio: The relationship of a borrower's monthly payment obligation on long-term debts divided by gross monthly income, expressed as a percentage. It is also known as bottom ratio.

Declaration: The master deed containing legal description of the condominium facility, a plat of the property, plans and specifications for the building and units, a description of the common areas, and the degree of ownership in the common areas available to each owner.

Declaration of Restrictions: The instrument used to record restrictive covenants on public record.

Dedication: An appropriation of land or an easement by the owner to the public.

Dedication by Deed: The deeding of a parcel of land to a municipality.

Deductible Expenses: The costs of operating property held for use in business or as an investment.

Deed: A written instrument transferring an interest in real property when delivered to the grantee.

Deed in Lieu of Foreclosure: The conveyance of title to the mortgagee by a mortgagor in default to avoid a record of foreclosure.

Deed Restriction: A limitation on land use appearing in a deed. For flippers, this may mean that the property cannot be resold again for a specified period of time, sometimes 6 months or longer.

Default: An act performed by the buyer, seller, tenant or landlord that breaches the contract of sale or lease and permits a claim for damages.

Defeasance Clause: A statement in a mortgage or deed of trust giving the borrower the right to redeem the title and have the mortgage lien released at any time prior to defaulting by paying the debt in full.

Defeasible Fee: A title subject to being revoked if certain conditions occur.

Deficiency Judgment: A court judgment obtained by a mortgagee for the amount of money a foreclosure sale proceed was deficient in fully satisfying the mortgage debt.

Delivery and Acceptance: This happens when the transfer of a title by deed is given by the grantor to the grantee.

Department of Housing and Urban Development/HUD or U.S. Department of Housing and Urban Development: A federal agency that administers funding for projects related to housing.

Depreciation: The expensing of the original cost of an asset, plus any qualified improvements, over its scheduled life as defined by the IRS. Depreciation deductions are permitted only for assets held by the production of income or used in a trade or business.

Descent: The distribution of property to qualified heirs of someone who has died intestate.

Description by Monument: The legal description of multiple-acre tracts of land and may refer to permanent objects such as a stone wall, large trees or boulders.

Description by Reference: A description on a deed that refers to a plat of subdivision or other legal document.

Devise: A gift of real property by will.

Disclosure and Informed Consent: A real estate agent explaining his or her position in the agency relationship and the verbal and written consent of the relationship by the client.

Disclosure Statement: An accounting of all financial aspects of a mortgage loan required of lenders to borrowers in residential mortgage loan as regulated by the Federal Reserve Board.

Discount Points: A one-time payment by the borrower to the lender at closing to obtain a lower interest rate on the mortgage loan. One point equals 1% of the loan amount; therefore, two points on a $100,000 mortgage would cost $2,000. It is also referred to as points.

Distribution Box: Part of a septic system that distributes the flow from the septic tank evenly to the absorption field or seepage pits.

Dominant Tenement: The land benefiting from an easement appurtenant.

Down Payment: The amount of money a buyer pays upfront in order to purchase a property

Dower: Dower is the part of or interest in the real estate of a deceased husband given by law to his widow during her life.

Dual Agent: A broker or salesperson who represents both the buyer and seller in the same transaction.

Due Diligence: The investigation and review of a property to determine any legal liability.

Duplex Apartment: An apartment consisting of two levels.

E.M.D.: Acronym for "earnest money deposit".

Earnest Money Deposit or EMD: Earnest money deposit is the deposit a buyer makes at the time of submitting an offer to demonstrate the true intent to purchase. It is also called a binder or good faith deposit.

Easement: A non-possessory right of the use of land.

Easement Appurtenant: A right of use in the adjoining land of another that moves with the title to the property benefiting from the easement.

Easement by Condemnation: Exercising the right of eminent domain.

Easement by Grant: Created by the express written agreement of the landowners, usually in a deed.

Easement in Gross: The right of use of the land of another without the requirement that the holder of the right own adjoining land.

Eave: The lowest part of the roof that projects beyond the walls of the structure.

Economic Depreciation: The physical deterioration of property caused by normal use, damage caused by natural or other hazards, and failure to adequately maintain property.

Economic Life: The period of time during which property is financially beneficial to an owner.

Effective Interest Rate: The actual rate of interest paid on a loan.

Egress: The exit from a building or parcel of land.

Enabling Acts: Laws passed by state legislatures authorizing cities and counties to regulate land use within their jurisdictions.

Encroachment: The trespassing on the land of another by a structure or other object.

Encumbrance: A claim, lien, charge or liability attached to and binding upon real property.

Environment Impact Statement or EIS: A requirement of the State Environmental Quality Review Act prior to initiating or changing a land use that may have an adverse effect on the environment.

Environmental Protection Agency or EPA: A federal agency that oversees land use.

Equal Credit Opportunity Act or ECOA: A federal law prohibiting discrimination in consumer laws.

Equitable Title: An interest in real estate such that a court will take notice and protect the owner's rights.

Equity: The difference between what something is worth and any loan secured by the asset

Equity of Redemption: The borrower's right to redeem the title pledged or conveyed in a mortgage or deed of trust after default and prior to a foreclosure sale by paying the debt in full, accrued interest and the lender's costs.

Erosion: The wearing away of land by water, wind or other processes of nature.

Escheat: The right of the government to take title to property left by a person who dies without leaving a valid will (intestate) or qualified heirs.

Escrow: A state where consideration, benefits, legal rights, document, or a sum of money is held by one person in trust for another, for the purpose of assuring performance under an agreement and for residential real estate sale this is usually the seller's attorney.

Escrow Agent: The person or entity that holds property in trust for third parties while a transaction is being finalized or a dispute is being resolved.

Estate: The collection of all assets of a deceased person. It is also the extent of interest a person has in real property.

Estate at Sufferance: The continuation to occupy property after legal authorization has expired.

Estate at Will: A leasehold condition that may be terminated at any point by either party.

Estate for Life: The interest of real property that ends with the death of a person.

Estate for Years: A leasehold condition of definite duration.

Estate from Year-to-Year: A leasehold state that automatically renews itself for consecutive periods until terminated by notice by either party. It is also called estate from period-to-period or periodic tenancy.

Estate in Real Property: An interest sufficient to provide the right to use, possession, and control of land. It also establishes the degree and duration of ownership.

Estoppel Certificate: A document executed by a mortgagor or mortgagee setting forth the principal amount and the executing parties are bound by the amount specified.

Express Agency: A relationship created by an oral or written agreement between a principal and an agent.

Eviction: A landlord's action that interferes with the tenant's use or possession of the property.

Exclusive Agency Agreement or Exclusive Listing: An agreement between a broker and a seller designating the broker as the seller's sole agent for the purpose of selling his or her property.

Exclusive Right To Sell Agreement: An agreement between a broker and a seller designating the broker as the seller's sole representative for the purpose of selling property. A commission is due to the broker even if the apartment is sold directly by the owner.

Exclusive Use Zoning: A type of zoning in which only the specified use may be made of property within the zoned district.

Executed Contract: An agreement that has been fully performed.

F.D.R.: Acronym for "formal dining room".

F.H.A Insured Loan: A mortgage insured by the Federal Housing Administration.

F.S.B.O.: Acronym for "For sale by owner".

Fair Housing Act of 1968: A federal act prohibiting discrimination in the sale, rental or financing of housing on the basis of race, color, religion, gender or national origin.

Fair Housing Act of 1988: A federal act that prohibits discrimination in the sale, rental, financing, or appraisal of housing on the basis of race, color, religion, gender, national origin, handicap, or familial status.

Fair Housing Amendments Act of 1988: An amendment to the Fair Housing Act that prohibits discrimination based on a mental or physical handicap, or family status.

Fair Market Value: The price for a property agreed upon between a buyer and seller in a competitive market.

Fannie Mae: Fannie Mae is the nickname for the Federal National

Mortgage Association (FNMA), a privately owned corporation that purchase FHA, VA, and conventional mortgages.

Fascia: The fascia is the area facing the outside of a soffit in house construction.

Federal Housing Administration or FHA: A federal agency that is part of the Department of Housing and Urban Development (HUD) that sets policy for mortgage underwriting and provides insurance for residential mortgages.

Fee Simple Absolute: The inheritable estate in land providing the greatest interest of any form of title.

Finance Charge: The amount imposed on the borrower in a mortgage loan, consisting of origination fee, service charges, discount points, interest, credit report fees, and finders' fees.

Financing: A loan secured by personal property, such as real estate property. The stock and lease of a cooperative corporation also constitute such personal property, and a loan secured by these instruments is referred to as a financing loan. Generally referred to as mortgages because they operate in the same manner, even though technically they are not.

First Mortgage: A mortgage whose lien is superior to the lien of any other mortgage on the same property because it was recorded prior to all other mortgages.

Fixed Lease: The rental amount remains the same for the entire lease term; also called flat, straight or gross lease.

Fixed-Rate Mortgage: A loan secured by real estate that has a fixed interest rate and payment amount for the term of the loan.

Fixture: An item that is permanently attached to a property.

Flashing: A metal material used in parts of the roof or walls to prevent water from penetrating the structure.

Flip Tax: A levy issued on the transfer of ownership by a cooperative corporation or condominium association against the seller, typically, though it may be against the buyer.

Floating Rate: A type of loan where the interest rate is not fixed over the term but is allowed to vary according to the change in a specified index, and is also referred to as an ARM or Adjustable Rate Mortgage.

Floating Slab: A type of foundation constructed by pouring the footing first and then pouring the slab after the footing has set.

Footing: The concrete base below the frost line that supports the foundation of the structure.

Foreclosure: An enforcement process in which the lender takes title to the property for the purposes of selling it to recoup money owed under the mortgage when it is defaulted.

Freddie Mac: The nickname for Federal Home Loan Mortgage Corporation (FHLMC), a corporation wholly owned by the Federal Home Loan Bank System that purchases FHA, VA, and conventional mortgages.

Frieze Board: The wood fastened under the soffit against a wall.

Front Foot: A linear foot of property frontage on a street or highway.

Full Bath: A bathroom that consists of a sink, toilet, and a bathtub or shower which could be separate or together.

Fully Amortizing Mortgage: A mortgage with scheduled uniform payments that will fully pay-off the loan over the term of the mortgage.

Functional Obsolescence: A flawed or faulty property that is rendered inferior because of advances or changes.

Gar: Acronym for garage.

General Agent: The entity that has full authority over a property of the principal, such as a property manager.

General Lien: A lien that attaches to all of the property of a person within the court's jurisdiction.

General Warranty Deed: A deed denoting an unlimited guarantee of title.

Ginnie Mae: The nickname for Government National Mortgage Association (GNMA), a U.S. government agency that purchases FHA and VA mortgages.

Girder: The main beam in a structure that spans the distance from one side of the foundation to the other.

Good Faith Estimate: An estimate of the fees a mortgage borrower will be required to pay at closing and is required by Federal law to be provided by the lender within three business days of the initial loan application.

Grace Period: In a mortgage, this refers to a specified time frame in which payment may be made without the borrower being in default.

Graduated Lease: A lease in which the rent changes from period to period over the lease term.

Graduated Payment Mortgage or GPM: Has payments that are lower in the early years but increase on a scheduled basis until they reach a level of amortization.

Grandfather Clause: Allows an activity to continue that was once considered acceptable or legal, but has since had the rules or laws changed.

Grant: A transfer of title to real property by deed.

Gross Lease: A lease in which the lessor pays all costs of operating and maintaining property, including the property taxes.

Ground Lease: A long-term lease of unimproved land and is usually for construction purposes.

H.O.A.: Acronym for Home Owner's Association.

H.U.D: Also known as the U.S. Department of Housing and Urban Development: A federal agency that administers funding for projects related to housing and oversees the home mortgage lending practices.

H.V.A.C: HVAC is an acronym that stands for heating, ventilation and air conditioning.

H.W.F.: Acronym for "hard wood floors".

H.W.T.: Acronym for "hot water tank".

Habendum Clause: The statement in a deed that begins with the words "to have and to hold" and describes the estate granted.

Half Bath: A room with a sink and toilet, but does not have a bathtub or shower.

Hazard Insurance: Insurance that covers unintentional damage by fire, smoke, wind, hail, theft, vandalism or other similar events.

Headers: Wooden reinforcements for the placement of doors and windows.

Holding Period: The length of time a property is owned.

Holdover Tenant: A tenant that remains in possession of a property after a lease terminates.

Home Equity Loan: A loan made against the equity in a home.

House Rules: Building rules regulating the conduct and responsibilities of homeowners as they affect the building's common areas and services.

Housing Expense Ratio: The relationship of a borrower's monthly payment obligation on housing (principal, interest, taxes, insurances and other applicable housing expenses) divided by gross monthly income, expressed as a percentage. It is also referred to as top ratio.

Hydronic System: Process in an HVAC system where liquids are heated or cooled.

Hypothecate: Pledge property as security for the payment of a debt without giving up possession.

Improvements: Changes or additions made to a property

Index: A benchmark, usually a published interest rate, such as a one-year London Interbank Offered Rate (LIBOR) security yields, used to calculate the interest rate of an adjustable rate mortgage when rate is scheduled to change.

Index Lease: A lease with a method of determining rent by an index.

Ingress: The right to enter a parcel of land, usually used as "ingress and egress", or both entering and leaving.

Injunction: A court instruction to discontinue a specified activity.

Insider Rights: Special rights offered to tenants occupying apartments in a building in the process of converting to a co-op or condo, giving them the exclusive right to buy their apartments for a limited period of time and normally at a discounted price.

Inspection: An examination of a property by a qualified inspector or engineer to understand the condition and to check for structural damage, termites, any required repairs or equipment replacement, etc.

Installment Land Contract or Contract for Deed: A contract of sale and a financing instrument wherein the seller agrees to convey title when the buyer completes the purchase price installment payments and is also called an installment land contract and installment plan.

Installment Sale: A property sale in which the purchaser pays the purchase price over a period of years.

Insurable Interest: The amount of property qualifying for insurance.

Insured Value: The amount that a structure is insured and should include the cost of replacing the structure if completely destroyed.

Interest Rates: The cost of borrowing money from a lender.

Interim Financing: A short-term or temporary loan such as a construction or bridge loan.

Interim Interest: Interest owed by the borrower to the lender on the mortgage loan from the day of the closing top the date covered by the first payment.

Intestate: The condition that occurs when someone dies without a valid will.

Involuntary Alienation: The transfer of title to real property as a result of a lien foreclosure sale, adverse possession, filing a petition in bankruptcy, condemnation under power of eminent domain, or upon the death of the titleholder to the state if there aren't any heirs.

J-51: A New York City program giving tax breaks for the substantial rehabilitation of an existing property. The program provides for an abatement of tax on a formula based on the level of improvement and an exclusion from additional tax due to the change in use of the property.

Joint Tenancy: A form of co-ownership that includes the right of survivorship.

Joist: A wooden framing member used in the construction of floors and ceilings.

Judgment Lien: A general lien resulting from a court decree.

Jumbo Loan: A mortgage issued in an amount exceeding the threshold stipulated under Fannie Mae (FNMA) regulations for a conforming loan.

L.R.: Acronym for "living room".

Land Lease: A situation in which a building and other land improvement are rented for a term of years and at the end of the term, the right of possession is extinguished and reverts back to the landowner while the tenant loses any remaining equity interest in the property.

Landmark Status: The designation given to a building or neighborhood that is under government protection for purposes of preservation.

Landmarks Commission: A city governmental agency assigned responsibility for recommending properties and neighborhoods to be identified as landmarks and ensuring they are properly preserved.

Lease: A written agreement to rent a property or part of a property from an owner.

Letter of Adequacy: A letter, usually issued by a managing agent, found in the offering plan of a building converting to cooperative or condominium ownership affirming that the income and expenses are adequate to cover the costs of running the building.

Liability: A debt or claim that is owed.

LIBOR Index: Stands for "London Interbank Offered Rate", and is the average yield of interbank offered rates for one-year U.S. dollar-denominated deposits in the London market. LIBOR is a common index used as a benchmark for adjusting mortgage interest rates in adjustable-rate mortgages.

Lien: An encumbrance on property which acts as security for the payment of a debt or the performance of an obligation.

Lien Foreclosure Sale: The sale of property without consent of the owner, as ordered by a court or authorized by state law due to a debt resulting in a lien.

Life Estate: A freehold estate created for the duration of the life or lives of certain named persons. It is a non-inheritable estate.

Life Estate in Remainder: A form of life estate in which certain persons are designated to receive the title upon termination of the life tenancy.

Like-Kind Exchange: An exchange of similar property, as defined in the Internal Revenue Code that can be performed without recognition of taxable gain at the time of transfer.

Limited Liability Company: A type of organization that is similar to a partnership, in that recognition of income and expenses flow directly through to the owners for tax purposes, without a corporate tax, but still permits insulation from liability similar to that of a corporation.

Liquidated Damages: The agreed amount to be paid as compensation for a breach of contract.

Liquidity: The ability of assets that are readily convertible to cash.

Lis Pendens or Notice of Lis Pendens: Refers to a pending lawsuit.

Listing: The term used by brokers to market an property or apartment for sale or rent.

Listing Broker: Represents the interests of the seller or landlord in the sale or rental of his or her property.

Loan Commitment: The written obligation from a lending institution to provide a mortgage to a borrower.

Loan Origination Fee: The financing charge required by a lender.

Loan-to-Value Ratio or LTV: The mortgage amount divided by the lower of the purchase price or the appraised value of the property.

Lock-In or Rate Lock Agreement: An agreement by the lender guaranteeing the applicant a specified interest rate on the mortgage loan provided the loan closes within a set period of time.

Lockbox: A device that is affixed to a door handle allowing someone access to a property if they have the code. Modern ones today will maintain records for all entrances to a property designated by the code provided.

Loft: An open living space that was converted from commercial space to residential space usually with very high ceilings, large windows and open space.

Lot: A measured section of land.

M.L.S.: Acronym for "Multiple Listing Service".

Maintenance: The monthly charge levied on owners by a cooperative corporation to cover the building's operating costs, real estate taxes, and the debt service on the building's underlying mortgage.

Managing Agent: Commonly seen in cooperative and condominium buildings which are managed by an outside company, or managing agent, which is responsible for the building operations.

Mansion Tax: A New York State tax of 1% of the selling price levied on the buyer of any residence costing in excess of $1,000,000.

Market Value: An estimate of the price for a property in relation to the current real estate market.

Martin Act: A New York State law regulating the conversion of properties to cooperative or condominium ownership, and is also referred to as Section 352eee and 352eeee of New York State's General Business Law.

Master Deed: The instrument that legally establishes a condominium. It is also referred to as a condominium declaration.

Mechanic's Lien: A statutory lien available to anyone supplying labor or material to the construction of an improvement of land that has not been properly compensated.

Metes and Bounds: A system of land description with distances and directions.

Monolithic Slab: A type of foundation in which the footing and slab are poured at the same time.

Mortgage: A pledge of real estate collateral to secure a debt. It is also referred to as a deed of trust.

Mortgage Banker: A representative from an institution that performs services similar to those of a mortgage broker. However, a mortgage banker is also legally permitted to lend its own funds.

Mortgage Broker: A real estate professional who represents an array of banks seeking to issue mortgages meets with a customer, assists with the application, and facilitates the mortgage process on behalf of the borrower and the bank and is often paid a fee by the bank for this service.

Mortgage Insurance or Private Mortgage Insurance or PMI: Insurance that protects the lender in case the home buyer does not make their mortgage payments and is usually required if the down payment is less than 20%.

Mortgage Note: A document signed at closing which states the borrower's promise to re-pay a sum of money. The note states an interest rate and a fixed period of time (term) for repayment.

Mortgage Satisfaction: The full payment of a mortgage loan.

Mortgagee: The lender in a mortgage transaction.

Mortgagor: The borrower in a mortgage transaction.

Multiple Dwelling or Multi-family: A structure with two or more residential units.

Multiple Listing Service or MLS: A central service for real estate listings available to member brokers.

National Association of Realtors or NAR: The largest and most prominent trade organization for real estate brokers and agents.

Negative Amortization: This occurs when a loan permits the borrower to make a payment that is less than the full amount required to cover the interest charge on the open balance and the shortfall is added to the mortgage principal.

Negative Pledge: This happens when the condominium places restrictions on the unit deed and trust agreement restricting the right of an owner to finance a condominium unit for more than a specified amount.

Net Lease: Refers to a type of lease in which the tenant pays a fixed rent plus the operational costs of the property.

Net Listing: A method of establishing the listing broker's commission as the entire amount above specified new amount to

the seller. This method of establishing a broker's commission is illegal in many states.

Net Worth: Assets less liabilities.

Nonconforming Use: The utilization of land that does not conform to the zoning ordinance for the area.

Non-recourse Note: A type of note in which the borrower has no personal liability for payment.

Notarize: Process of having a certified Notary Public to verify the authenticity of a signature.

Notice of Lis Pendens: A public record warning all concerned parties that title to a property is the subject of a lawsuit and any lien resulting from the suit will attaché to the title.

Offer: An offer is made to purchase a property at a specific price

Offering Plan or Prospectus: A document issued by a sponsor in the process of converting a building to a cooperative or condominium ownership. It is intended to provide full disclosure of all relevant facts associated with evaluating an investment in the property, and is also referred to as the offering plan or black book.

Open-ended Listing Contract: A contract between a seller and a real estate broker that does not have a termination date.

Open-end Mortgage: A mortgage that may be refinanced without rewriting the mortgage contract.

Origination: The first step in the mortgage loan process consisting of the completion of the application.

Ordinance: A law enacted by the local government.

Open Listing: An apartment for sale for which the owner has not signed an exclusive agreement with a real estate broker.

Option to Renew: A provision in a lease that states the method and terms of a lease renewal.

Origination Fee: A service charge by a lending institution for a mortgage.

Ownership in Severalty: The title to real property held in the name of one person only.

Parcel: A specific portion of land such as a lot.

Partition: The legal proceeding that divides property of co-owners so each will hold title in severalty.

Party Wall: The wall in common between two adjoining structures, such as in townhouses and brownstones.

Passive Loss: A loss generated by investment real estate when real estate is not the taxpayer's primary business.

Penthouse: The apartment on the highest floor in a luxury, high-rise building.

Percentage Lease: A lease that has a rental amount that is a combination of a fixed amount plus a percentage of the lessee's gross sales.

Percolation: The movement of water through soil.

Percolation or Perc Test: A test to determine if the soil is sufficient for the installation of a septic tank.

Perfecting a Loan: When a loan is issued against a personal property, it is recorded in the county clerk's office against the name of the borrower. The recording process perfects a security position against the collateral.

Periodic Tenancy: A lease automatically renews for successive periods unless terminated by either party.

Phantom Gain: A sale of real estate in which income is recognized for tax purposes but no money has been received correlating to the gain amount. This can occur when the property's basis has been depreciated below the property's mortgage amount.

Pied-a-Terre: A term that refers to an apartment that is not the primary residence of the owner and only used sporadically throughout the year.

PITI: An acronym for a mortgage payment that includes principal, interest, taxes and insurance.

Plat: A property map that is part of the public record.

Platform Framing: The most common type of framing in residential construction in which the framing of the structure rests on a subfloor platform.

Points: The payment made to a lender as consideration for issuing a mortgage, usually based on a percentage of the loan amount. Each point is equal to 1% of the principal of the mortgage.

Post-War: A post-war building is one that was built after World War II, typically between the 1950s and 1970s. They vary in size, but are usually taller than pre-war buildings, are often constructed of white, red or brown brick and have few architectural details. The rents are usually lower than in pre-war or newer buildings.

Powder Room: A half-bath having only a toilet and sink.

Pre-Approval: A process in which a conditional commitment is issued after a loan profile is underwritten with all standard documentation except a property appraisal and a title search.

Pre-Qualification: A process in which a loan officer calculates the housing-to-income ratio and the total debt-to-income ratio to determine an approximate maximum mortgage loan amount.

Pre-War Building: Built before World War II, and mainly prior to 1929, since there were few residential buildings built during the 1930s. Buildings are less than 20 stories and usually have large rooms, mouldings, hardwood floors and high ceilings.

Price-to-Earnings Ratio or P/ Ratio: The metric used to assess the relative valuation of equities.

Price-to-Income Ratio: It is the basic affordability measure for housing in a given area and is the ratio of median house prices to median familial disposable incomes, expressed as a percentage or as years of income. This ratio, applied to individuals, and also referred to as attainability and is a basic component of mortgage lending decisions.

Price-Rent Ratio: The average cost of ownership divided by the received rent income (if buying to let) or the estimated rent that would be paid if renting (if buying to reside).

Primary Residence: Generally, is someone considered to occupy the property the majority of the time and typically defined as 6 months and 1 day per year at minimum.

Principal: The principal in the mortgage is the amount that is borrowed and on which interest is paid or received.

Private Mortgage Insurance or PMI: The insurance that protects the lender in case the home buyer does not make their mortgage payments. Typically, a borrower would be required to pay this if their down payment is less than 20%.

Processing: Processing is the second step in the mortgage application process which involves the verification of information stated on the application. Credit reports and the appraisal are also ordered at this time.

Property Condition Disclosure Form: This form is a comprehensive checklist pertaining to the condition of the property including its structure and any environmental issues in and around the property.

Property Description: The accurate, legal description of the land.

Property Tax: The tax issued by a municipality on the ownership of a property.

Proprietary Lease: The lease issued by a cooperative corporation to each tenant-shareholder prescribing his or her right to occupy a specific apartment and his or her general obligations as an owner and tenant.

Pro-Rata Share: In relation to a co-op, the pro-rata share is your apartment's share of the building's underlying mortgage. The share is determined by dividing the amount of the underlying mortgage by the number of shares in the building then multiplying the per-share amount by the number of shares for your apartment. The lower of either the appraised value or purchase price then divides that number.

Prospectus: A document issued by a sponsor in the process of converting a building to a cooperative or condominium ownership. It is intended to provide "full disclosure" of all relevant facts associated with evaluating an investment in the property, and is also referred to as the offering plan or black book.

Quadruplex: An apartment with four levels.

R.E.O.: Acronym for Real Estate Owned meaning a bank has taken title to a property and this usually happens when properties are foreclosed on.

Radon: Radon is a colorless, odorless gas present in soil that enters a home through small spaces and openings.

Rate Cap: The limit on interest rates during the term of an adjustable rate mortgage.

Rate Lock: An agreement between the borrower and the mortgage lender that guarantees a rate for a set period of time (typically 30, 60 or 90 days).

Ratios: Guidelines applied by the lender during underwriting a mortgage loan application to determine how large a loan to grant an applicant. The ratios the lenders use are generally the Loan-to-Value Ratio, Housing-to-Income Ratio, and Debt-to-Income ratio.

Real Estate Broker: An individual employed on a fee or commission basis as an agent to bring buyers and sellers together and assist in negotiating real estate contracts between them. A broker has continued their education beyond that which is required of a real estate agent and is also able to work independently or have agents working for them.

Real Estate Investment Trust or REIT: A trust owned by shareholders that buys and initiates mortgage loans.

Real Estate Salesperson or Agent: A salesperson performs any of the acts of a real estate broker but while associated with and supervised by a broker.

Real Estate Settlement Procedures Act or RESPA: A federal law that regulates the activities of lending institutions in making mortgage loans.

Real Property Tax Lien: This lien is a tax levied against real property by the local government and has priority over all other liens.

Realtor: A real estate agent who is a member of the National Association of Realtors. As a member, the agent must agree to abide by the associations standards and uphold the code of ethics.

Recognition Letter: A letter is a letter from the cooperative corporation's board of directors recognizing the secured rights of a lender to the shares of stock and the proprietary lease on a specific apartment.

Recording: Registering the ownership, lien, or claim of a party to a specific parcel of real estate with the local county.

Recording Fees: The fees charged by the recorder's office to record a document such as a mortgage, deed of trust, deed and UCC Financing Statement.

Redlining: The resistance of lending institutions to make loans for the purchase, construction, or repair of a dwelling due to the socio-economic conditions of the property's location. Literally in the past, bankers would red line maps to indicate which areas that they did not want to provide lending.

Referral Fee: A percentage of a broker's commission paid to another broker for the referral of a buyer or seller.

Refinancing: Using the proceeds of a new loan used to pay off an existing mortgage on the same property.

Rental: The possession, but not ownership, of a property for a limited duration of time under defined terms and conditions.

Rental Building: A rental building only has apartments for rent and not for purchase.

Rent Control: A form of rent regulation, rent control occurs when an apartment has tenants that have been in continual residence since July 1, 1971, or other qualified occupants that have been in residence with the original tenant continuously for either two years (immediate relative) or five years (non-relative). Rent control limits the amount of rent landlords can charge for apartments and restricts their ability to evict.

Rent Stabilization: Another form of rent regulation, rent stabilization usually applies to buildings built before 1974 and apartments removed from rent control. After the rent has legally been raised to over $2,500 per month, or the household income of the tenants is over $200,000 per year, rent stabilization is no longer in effect. The amount that landlords are legally allowed to increase the rent every year is regulated by the NYC Rent Guidelines Board. It also covers buildings that receive J-51 and 421-A tax benefits, so there are newer buildings with apartments that have higher rent that also are regulated by rent stabilization.

Reserve Fund: The amount reserved to provide funds for future expenses in order to maintain a cooperative or condominium building and is managed by the building's board.

Residential Lead-based Paint Hazard Reduction Act: This act stipulates procedures to be followed in disclosing the presence of lead-based paint in the sale or rental of properties built prior to 1978.

Reverse Annuity Mortgage: A type of mortgage that retirees on fixed incomes can use to generate income out of the equity in their homes while they continue to live in the home.

R-Factor or R-Value: A rating that measures the degree of resistance to heat transfer.

Rider: An addendum to a document that covers supplemental issues.

Ridge Beam: The highest part of framing in a structure and forms the apex of the roof.

Right of Assignment: The right of assignment allows the lender to sell a mortgage at any time and obtain money invested rather than wait for the completion of the loan term.

Right of First Refusal: A condition contained in many

condominium master deeds that permits the board to review any party seeking to purchase or rent an apartment and to refuse the applicant if it so desires. If the board refuses the applicant, it must thereafter purchase or rent the apartment under the same terms and conditions stipulated in the contract.

Right of Survivorship: The right of an owner to receive the title to a co-owner's share upon death of the co-owner, as in the case of joint tenancy and tenancy by the entirety.

Right-of-Way: An easement allowing someone to use the land of another for a specific purpose.

Riparian Rights: The rights of an owner of property adjoining a watercourse such as a river, including access to and use of the water.

Running with the Land: Refers to rights that are passed with the title of property and ownership stays with the land rather than the land owner.

Sale Price: The purchase price, refers to the amount of money paid by the purchaser to the seller.

Sales Comparison Approach: An appraisal tool for estimating the value of a property with other similar properties that have sold recently.

Satisfaction of Mortgage: Indicates the mortgage has been paid in full.

Schedule A: A list in the offering plan of all the apartments being sold in a newly-constructed building or one that is undergoing conversion. It presents allocated shares or unit-percentage interest, room count, and other material cost elements, including the projected maintenance charge and the tax-deductible portion of the maintenance.

Schedule B: The projected cost of operating a cooperative or condominium during its first year of operation and is part of the offering plan.

Section 421 A: A New York City tax program intended to stimulate new construction by permitting a phase-in of the real estate tax over a period of ten years.

Security Deposit: The payment required by the landlord that guarantees that the tenant will meet their financial obligations under the terms of the lease. Besides guarding against any unpaid rent, it also guards against any potential damage that may be incurred by the tenant.

Seller Contribution: A payment by the seller of a property of some, or all, of the buyer's closing costs.

Seller's Agent: The listing agent that works in the best interests of the seller.

Service Drop: The above-ground electrical cables that come from the nearest electrical pole connecting the electrical service of the house.

Service Lateral: The underground electrical wiring connecting the electrical service of the house.

Servicing: Servicing are activities the lender performs such as collecting the payments and/or paying taxes and insurance from an escrow account.

Servient Tenement : The land encumbered by an easement.

Setback: The distance from the front or interior property line to the point where the structure is located.

Severalty: Ownership by only one person.

Shares: When purchasing in a cooperative building, the apartment is not actually purchased directly as real estate but rather shares in the cooperative corporation are purchased. The amount of shares represent the portion of the building owned based on the size and location of the unit in the apartment. A proprietary lease is then issued by the corporation for a specific unit to the purchaser.

Short Sale: A sale of real estate in which the proceeds of the sale will not be sufficient to cover the liens and loans on the property. The financial institution must agree to the sale in order for the sale to go through.

Single Family: Free standing residential building.

Soffit: The area under the roof extension of a structure that can be made of wood, vinyl or aluminum.

SONYMA or Sonny Mae: SONYMA or State of New York Mortgage Agency raises money from the sale of New York tax-free bonds and uses these funds for mortgage loans.

Sponsor: The developer or owner of the property that initiates the conversion of a property from single ownership to cooperative or condominium ownership.

Square Footage: The area measured in square feet of a certain property. Square footage can be measured in different ways and is usually considered approximate. Condominium apartments have specific laws that determine the way in which the apartment is measured and usually more accurately reflect the actual square footage within a property.

Standing Mortgage: An interest-only mortgage with no principal reduction over time. Refer to *Balloon Mortgage*.

Subject to Financing: A clause in the contract of sale for a cooperative apartment stipulating that the agreement is conditioned upon the buyer's obtaining financing from a financial institution in an agreed-upon amount.

Sublet: The owner of an apartment or the main lease holder decides to rent the apartment to a sub-tenant.

Super Jumbo Loan: This is a loan that exceeds $1,000,000.

Survey: A document indicating measurements, boundaries and the area of a property.

Tax Abatement: A financial incentive offered by a local or municipal government to stimulate development in a particular area. The owner of the property and/or the developer has reduced taxes for a specific period of time, typically 10-15 years. The taxes are raised incrementally to the full tax burden over the period of a few years.

Tax Deductible: Expense that helps to reduce taxable income.

Tenancy by the Entirety: Co-ownership limited to husband and wife, with the right to survivorship.

Tenancy in Common: A co-ownership that does not include the right of survivorship.

Term, Amortization: The period of time in which the interest and principal payments of a loan must be made.

Term Mortgage: A mortgage with interest payments only during the mortgage term, with the principal due at the end of the term.

Title: The evidence or documentation that an owner is in lawful possession of the property, such as a property deed.

Title Company: Ensures that the title to the real estate is legitimate and then issues title insurance for the property.

Title Insurance: An insurance policy protecting the insured from financial loss caused by a defect or question about the title to real property.

Title Search: A process that examines local public records, laws and related court decisions to determine if any other parties have valid claims against the subject property (such as past due taxes, judgments or mechanics' liens). It also discloses past and current facts about the subject property's ownership.

Title Transfer Tax: A tax imposed on the conveyance of title to real property by deed.

Townhouse: A private residence where at least one wall is shared with another residence.

Triple Mint Condition: Refers to a residence that is in immaculate condition.

Triple Net Lease: A condition when the lessee pays all the expenses associated with the property in addition to the rent.

Triplex: An apartment that has three levels.

Truth-in-Lending Disclosure: Federal law requires that the lender must give this document to the home buyer within three business days after the loan application. This disclosure gives details of the mortgage payments along with the corresponding APR and finance charges.

Underwriting: The decision-making process used to determine whether the loan risk is acceptable to the lender

Unencumbered Property: Property that is free of any lien.

Unity of Interest: Co-owners all have the same percentage of ownership in a property.

Unity of Possession: Co-owners have the right to possess any and all portions of the property owned, without physical division.

Unity of Time: Co-owners receive title at the same time in same conveyance.

Unity of Title: Co-owners have the same type of ownership in a property.

Unrelated Business Taxable Income or UBTI: A special federal tax levied on investment income generated from property held in a pension plan in which there is a mortgage. The property ownership is allocated between the cash investment and the mortgage, and all gain allocable to the mortgage portion is subject to UBTI tax.

Unsold Shares: Shares of stock in a cooperative corporation transferred to the sponsor at the completion of the conversion process.

U.S. Department of Housing and Urban Development or HUD: A federal agency that administers funding for projects related to housing and oversees the home mortgage lending practices.

Useful Life: Rhe period of time that a property is expected to be economically useful.

Use Variance: The permission to use the land for a purpose which, under the current zoning restrictions, is prohibited.

Usury: Charging a rate of interest higher than the rate allowed by law.

Vacancy Rate: The projected rate of the percentage of rental units that will be vacant in a given year.

VA Guaranteed Loan: A mortgage loan in which the loan payment is guaranteed to the lender by the Department of Veteran Affairs.

Valuation: Establishes an opinion of value utilizing an objective approach based on facts related to the property, such as age, square footage, location, cost to replace, etc.

Value in Use: The present worth of the future benefits of ownership.

Variance: A deviation from specific requirements of a zoning ordinance due to special conditions of the property.

Vendor's Affidavit: A document signed under oath by the seller stating that the seller has not encumbered title to real estate without full disclosure to the purchaser.

Vesting Options: Choices buyers have in how to acquire property.

Vicarious Liability: One person being responsible for the actions of another.

W.D.: Acronym for "washer and dryer".

W.I.C.: Acronym for "walk in closet".

Walk-up Building: A building that does not have an elevator and are usually four or five stories.

Walk-Through Inspection: Inspection that occurs shortly before a closing to ensure that the property is being delivered as stipulated in the contract of sale and is often referred to as the final inspection.

Wetlands: Federal and state protected transition areas between uplands and aquatic habitats that provide flood and storm water control, surface and groundwater protection, erosion control, and pollution treatment.

Words of Conveyance: A stipulation in a deed demonstrating the definite intent to convey a specific title to real property to a named grantee.

Wraparound Mortgage: A junior mortgage in an amount exceeding a first mortgage against the property.

Writ of Attachment: A court order preventing any transfer of attached property during litigation.

Yield: The return on an investment.

Zone: An area of a municipality or specific building that is designated for a specific use, such as residential, commercial, etc.

Zoning: Laws regulating land use.

Zoning Ordinance: A statement settling forth the type of use permitted under each zoning classification and specific requirements for compliance.

What Do They Really Mean?

Realtors are sales people. They're paid to see the best in properties and get others to see beyond the obvious. They're paid to show the best of what a property has to offer and they are not there to point out problems. What happens is language is used to be creative and show the positive spin on properties. The problem with this is that the language can sometimes be misinterpreted by others viewing the same property.

This is not at all uncommon in any business. Think about meetings that are held in any work place. There could be 1 Meeting with 1 leader and 27 participants. Everyone's hearing the same thing, the same way, with the same voice inflection and body language and yet when the meeting is over, there will be 28 different versions of what was just said. Why is this? It's because people pay attention and apply their own perceptions. Some will take what's said at face value by the letter of what is said and not look for the spirit of what is said. Some may intently watch the leader looking for the hidden messages in what is being said. Another may be distracted with a personal issue. Someone else may be distracted because he or she is texting under the table or might not be feeling well. People generally seek out information that supports their beliefs and discount things that don't. Messages could get lost when any of these things happen. This is exactly why in a meeting of 27 people with one leader that there will be 28 versions of what was said.

This is not to say that realtors and people selling homes are being purposely deceptive. It is because they are paid to do a job and that job is to identify the positive aspects about a property and not everyone will agree on those positive aspects. Keep a good sense of humor reading through this section. So with real estate descriptions this is what *could* happen:

If they say this........	*They could mean this........*
The house is cozy.	The house is small.
It's charming.	The house is old and quirky.
There are great neighbors.	They might be in your business.
Offered as-is.	Could mean serious problems.
Damp basement in the spring.	Could mean feet of water.
Easy access to everywhere.	Located near the highway.
Fixer upper.	Best off getting an inspection.
Mature Landscaping.	Needs lots of weeding.
Single owner.	Probably hasn't been updated.
Short Sale.	Don't expect to move soon.
Deed Restriction.	Your stay will be longer.
Unique Design.	Unusual layout. Lots of character.

The 4 Step Flip! Maria A. Mendez, MBA

There's a water view.	It may not be from the windows.
It is on the waterfront.	Could be a pond in the yard.
It's practical.	Functional, but nothing special.
It has great potential.	Get ready to redecorate.
Updated electrical.	A new outlet was put in.
Updated plumbing.	A pipe was replaced.
It's filled with natural light.	It is lacking light fixtures.
Completely updated.	It was painted throughout.
Luxury....state of the art.	Not affordable to most.
Great for students!	"Over" charging by the bedroom.
Great for students!	Could be near a college.
Move in ready.	No one has lived there in awhile.
Conveniently located.	Lots of traffic and noise nearby.
Easily maintained.	Very small living space.
Reduced price.	Probably overpriced initially.
Reduced price.	Bid at list price or higher.
Motivated seller.	Bidding opportunities.

Motivated seller.	Desperate seller.
Near schools.	Lots of traffic at school times.
Near schools.	Your driveway=their hangout.
Must see inside.	No curb appeal.
Subject to 3rd party approval.	Probably a short sale.
As is.	Don't ask for seller concessions.
As is.	May need repairs.
Cash buyers only.	Can't get a bank mortgage.
Photos not available.	The inside is hideous.
Stunning and spectacular.	Hopelessly average.

The lesson here is to not believe everything you read and also, not to believe everything you see. Some pictures of properties may have been taken a decade ago and not truly reflect the existing condition. So do your due diligence, and use your imagination as you read through the listings.

AUTHOR BIOGRAPHY

Maria was born, raised and lives with her family in the Western NY area. Her son, Dominic, is the light of her life. Her grandparents immigrated here from Germany, Ireland and Mexico and therefore, Maria represents a true piece of America, a melting pot. It was a very different time then as diversity was not celebrated. When people immigrated to America, they believed that they should assimilate to the American customs and way of life.

Maria studied at the State University of New York at Buffalo and obtained a BS in Business with concentrations in Human Resource Management and Marketing while also obtaining a BA in Psychology. She furthered her education by obtaining her MBA in Human Resource Management. Maria also obtained an Accelerated Banking Certificate from the American Institute of Banking as well as an ICA Certificate in Anti-Money Laundering and Sanctions Compliance from the International Compliance Association. Maria had spent nearly 25 years working in Commercial Banking at a fortune 500 company before entering the next phase of her life.

In addition to becoming an author, Maria was ordained as a reverend. Keeping in line with focusing on small businesses, she also plans events to provide a platform for small businesses to sell their items. Maria is also a student of the universe and believes there are always opportunities to learn, even outside of formal education. Maria believes that true success is about more than money, titles and status. It's about having an enriched life and making an impact. One of the only ways to have an enriched life is to give back to the community. Maria is deeply committed to helping people become more resilient so they can thrive in life, be more productive and lives that they want to live with more balance and purpose.

Maria is a believer of education and shaping young minds. She has been active in the community and is currently a judge for the Forever a Phoenix and Paying it forward Scholarships at the University of Phoenix, a judge for the INVESTWRITE stock market competition for SIFMA and has been a Professional Business Tutor, Mentor and Coach at Villa Maria College. She also is a Business Consultant and has helped small businesses get up and running. Maria has also served as a Chemo Angel for those with life threatening or terminal cancer and since she is an animal lover she has served as a foster mom with the SPCA. Her passion for helping people has been exemplified in all areas of her life. Maria is always looking for new opportunities to get involved.

Maria's interest in real estate started back in the mid 1990's when she accepted a position in Commercial Real Estate Loan Administration at a Fortune 500 financial institution. This is where she started to learn about purchasing properties at delinquent tax sales. Her first flip property was closed in 2007 and she formalized the endeavor with the creation of Stone Point Investment Group which quickly grew and expanded to the creation of Stone Point Development Group, LLC. In addition to flipping and renovating properties, Stone Point also provides consumer education. Subscribe to Maria's YouTube Channel, Stone Point Investment Group, to see the short educational videos.

For those who wish to contact Maria with questions, comments or business interests (speaking engagements, book signings, becoming a certified speaker on the book's content, one on one coaching, etc), email is the best option. She can be reached at stonepointinvestment@gmail.com or mmendez2727@gmail.com.

OTHER BOOKS BY THE AUTHOR

Flipping Secrets. A follow up book to **The 4 Step Flip** expanding on what one tells you about flipping real estate. Coming in late 2018 or 2019.

Get Out of Your Way! A book about what holds us back and how to move forward.

101 Things To Do To Get Out of Your Way. A follow up book to Get Out of Your Way to help get you started on your journey and life transformation. Coming late in218 or 2019.

DEDICATION TO READERS

I hope that you've enjoyed reading The 4 Step Flip! Some people are happy working day jobs for other people trading their time for money, but for those of you who aren't, hopefully have you've learned something new and recognize that ***you can quit your day job*** and start a career investing in real estate.

If you take a chance, you just might find that you could lead a more rewarding life and have a better work life balance by working for yourself in real estate.

Good luck with your real estate endeavors and Happy Flipping!

www.ingramcontent.com/pod-product-compliance
Lightning Source LLC
Chambersburg PA
CBHW071412220526
45469CB00004B/1266